Book of James Volume 2

Developing
A Faith
That Works

Taught by Pastor Rick Warren

PurposeDriven®

Published by Purpose Driven® Publishing.
20 Empire
Lake Forest, CA 92630
www.purposedriven.com

TABLE OF CONTENTS

You have just opened up a power tool. It doesn't look like a tool, it doesn't feel like a tool, and it doesn't have a power cord, but it's definitely a tool! This tool was designed for you, an ordinary Christian—the kind of Christian who sincerely desires to live for God and yet struggles to stay on track. If you are the kind of Christian whose life is fast-paced and full but not always fulfilled, this tool is for you.

This curriculum tool is like any tool: it needs to be used. Put this tool into action and it will be productive in your life and in your group. The Purpose Driven® Bible Study Series may have a few features that are new to you, but we encourage you to give them a try. A tool is most effective when used for its intended purpose. This curriculum tool has three intended purposes.

1. Digging Deeper Into the Word of God

Each of the six lessons in this curriculum includes study of at least one core Bible passage. This interactive study not only allows for discussion of the passage, but also provides opportunity to discuss practical application as a response to the passage. Tremendous spiritual power is experienced when a group wrestles with not only the meaning of a passage but also its meaning for their lives.

2. Building Community

No Christ-follower was intended to live in isolation. The Bible speaks nothing of "lone ranger" faith, but more than fifty times in the New Testament, God speaks of a "one another" type of faith. One of the great benefits of group life is that it provides you with a practical laboratory in which to experience New Testament community. In group life you find a place to belong and people with whom to share your life.

3. Sharpening Your Focus on God's Purposes

One unique feature of this tool is that it seeks to balance all five purposes of God in your group experience. Without an intentional focus on including all five purposes, most groups focus on fellowship or become a Bible study group only. This study is designed to help create and nurture a hunger and passion to live out all God's purposes for his children.

So, pick it up. Don't be afraid of it. Use it. Allow it to stretch and challenge you. God has put your group together and he wants to use each member in your life. He wants to use you in their lives as well. So pray for your group and come to your group time ready to participate. May you build a life that is pleasing to God.

Outline of Each Session

You are about to embark on a life-changing experience in your small group. Studying God's Word together with other believers always impacts our lives in ways we can't imagine.

As your group studies the Bible together, this study guide will help you strengthen and deepen God's five purposes for your lives. One of the unique features of this curriculum is that it uses the five purposes as the format for each session. When you see the following symbols and elements in the study guide, you will know the particular purpose that section promotes. The format of each session is as follows:

Connect (Fellowship) — Intimate connection with God and his family is the foundation for spiritual growth. The questions in this section will help you get to know the members of your group so you'll begin to feel a sense of belonging and family.

Grow (Discipleship) — Each week you will watch Pastor Rick Warren's teaching video for the session. We ask you to follow along using the teaching outline in your study guide and your Bible. After the teaching video, discuss the questions that follow. The questions are designed to facilitate a deeper understanding of the Bible and help you consider how the truths of the Bible can impact your life.

Serve (Ministry) — Nothing is more fulfilling than using your God-given gifts to serve and help meet the needs of others in God's family. This section will help make that desire a reality. You will be encouraged to discover your unique shape and challenged to take steps to serve those inside and outside your group.

Share (Evangelism) — The thought of sharing your faith can be scary and relationally awkward. Such feelings are common and understandable. But God can and wants to use you to reach those around you for Christ. This section is designed to give you and your group practical, manageable steps for sharing Christ that can become a part of your everyday life.

Worship — In each small group session you will have the opportunity to surrender your heart to God and express your worship to him. You will be introduced in this section to various forms of small group worship including prayer, singing together, and sharing what God is doing in your lives. This portion of your session can be very meaningful for your group. If singing and praying in a group is new to you, feel free to not participate until you feel comfortable.

Additional Study — If your group wants a little more Bible study and has the time, we provide a few additional questions to discuss. This is optional.

Preparation for Next Time —This section is for groups or individuals willing to do more study during the week. You could use these questions to go deeper biblically, reflect on the lesson, or record your thoughts in a journal. This section generally includes cross-references relevant to the subject you will study the coming week. It will also include questions and practical ideas for applying the upcoming week's lesson.

Memory Verse — In each session we provide a verse to memorize. While this may be a challenge for you, please take this opportunity to grow deeper in your walk with God through this key spiritual habit.

Host Tips — We have provided a number of questions in each section of the curriculum. As the host we encourage you to select the questions you believe are most beneficial for your group. If your group is unable to work through the entire curriculum, we have recommended a question or activity with an asterisk (*) in each section of the study. These brief instructions in gray type are helpful coaching hints for your group host. Here's your first tip . . .

> **HOST TIP:** THE STUDY GUIDE MATERIAL IS MEANT TO BE YOUR SERVANT, NOT YOUR MASTER. SO PLEASE DON'T FEEL YOU HAVE TO ANSWER EVERY QUESTION IN EVERY SECTION. THE POINT IS NOT TO RACE THROUGH THE SESSION; THE POINT IS TO TAKE TIME TO LET GOD WORK IN YOUR LIVES. NOR IS IT NECESSARY TO "GO AROUND THE CIRCLE" BEFORE YOU MOVE ON TO THE NEXT QUESTION. GIVE PEOPLE THE FREEDOM TO SPEAK, BUT DON'T INSIST THAT THEY DO. YOUR GROUP WILL ENJOY DEEPER, MORE OPEN SHARING AND DISCUSSION IF PEOPLE DON'T FEEL PRESSURED TO SPEAK UP. IF YOUR GROUP IS UNABLE TO WORK THROUGH ALL THE MATERIAL IN A SESSION, WE HAVE RECOMMENDED ONE QUESTION OR ACTIVITY WITH AN ASTERISK (*) IN EACH SECTION OF THE STUDY.

Follow these simple steps for a successful small group session:

1. Open your group meeting by using the "Connect" section in your study guide.

2. Watch Pastor Rick's video teaching and follow along in the outlines in the study guide. Each video lesson is about twenty minutes in length.

3. Complete the rest of the discussion materials for each session in the study guide.

It's just that simple. Have a great study together!

7

SESSION SEVEN:
HOW TO MANAGE
YOUR MOUTH

JAMES 3:1–12

Connect . . . . .15 minutes

> HOST TIP: IF YOUR GROUP IS UNABLE TO WORK THROUGH THE ENTIRE CURRICULUM, WE HAVE RECOMMENDED ONE
> QUESTION OR ACTIVITY WITH AN ASTERISK (*) IN EACH SECTION OF THE STUDY.

*1. Open to the *Purpose Driven Group Guidelines* in the *Small Group Resources* section of the study guide, page 72. Take a few minutes to review these group guidelines before you begin this second of a two-part series on the book of James. These guidelines will help everyone know what to expect from the group and how to contribute to a worthwhile study.

2. In this opening session on "How to Manage Your Mouth," Pastor Rick discusses the power of the tongue and problems it can present. Tell about a time when your mouth got you into a bit of trouble (maybe with your parents, your spouse, your boss, or even this group).

Grow . . . . .35–40 minutes

Memory Verse
Let the peace of Christ rule in your hearts . . .
Colossians 3:15a (NIV)

Watch the video now. Follow along in your Bibles and take notes on the provided outline.

¹Not many of you should presume to be teachers, my brothers, because you know that we who teach will be judged more strictly. ²We all stumble in many ways. If anyone is never at fault in what he says, he is a perfect man, able to keep his whole body in check. ³When we put bits into the mouths of horses to make them obey us, we can turn the whole animal. ⁴Or take ships as an example. Although they are so large and are driven by strong winds, they are steered by a very small rudder wherever the pilot wants to go. ⁵Likewise the tongue is a small part of the body, but it makes great boasts. Consider what a great forest is set on fire by a small spark. ⁶The tongue also is a fire, a world of evil among the parts of the body. It corrupts the whole person, sets the whole course of his life on fire, and is itself set on fire by hell. ⁷All kinds of animals, birds, reptiles and creatures of the sea are being tamed and have been tamed by man, ⁸but no man can tame the tongue. It is a restless evil, full of deadly poison. ⁹With the tongue we praise our Lord and Father, and with it we curse men, who have been made in God's likeness. ¹⁰Out of the same mouth come praise and cursing. My brothers, this should not be. ¹¹Can both fresh water and salt water flow from the same spring? ¹²My brothers, can a fig tree bear olives, or a grapevine bear figs? Neither can a salt spring produce fresh water. (James 3:1–12 NIV)

Why Must I Watch What I Say?

1. My tongue directs _____ where I go _____.

   When we put bits into the mouths of horses . . . we can turn the whole animal.
   (James 3:3 NIV)

   Or take ships as an example. Although they are so large and are driven by strong winds, they are steered by a very small rudder wherever the pilot wants to go.
   (James 3:4 NIV)

2. My tongue can destroy _____what I have_____ .

Likewise the tongue is a small part of the body, but it makes great boasts. Consider what a great forest is set on fire by a small spark. (James 3:5 NIV)

You will have to live with the consequences of everything you say. (Proverbs 18:20 GN)

The tongue also is a fire, a world of evil among the parts of the body. It corrupts the whole person, sets the whole course of his life on fire, and is itself set on fire by hell. (James 3:6 NIV)

All Hell broke loose.

⁷All kinds of animals, birds, reptiles and creatures of the sea are being tamed and have been tamed by man, ⁸but no man can tame the tongue. It is a restless evil, full of deadly poison. (James 3:7–8 NIV) assasinate reputations.

3. My tongue displays _____Who I Am._____ .

⁹With the tongue we praise our Lord and Father, and with it we curse men, who have been made in God's likeness. ¹⁰Out of the same mouth come praise and cursing. My brothers, this should not be. (James 3:9–10 NIV)

WHY YOU TALK THE WAY you do, it's inside you.

¹¹Can both fresh water and salt water flow from the same spring? ¹²My brothers, can a fig tree bear olives, or a grapevine bear figs? Neither can a salt spring produce fresh water. (James 3:11–12 NIV)

The problem is with _____your heart_____ .

What Is the Solution?

1. _____Get a new heart._____ .

Create in me a clean heart, O God . . . (Psalm 51:10a NASB)

2. _____Ask God for help everyday_____ .

3. _____Think before you speak_____ .

Everyone should be quick to listen, slow to speak and slow to become angry, . . . (James 1:19b NIV)

Discussion Questions

1. In James 3:1–12, what word pictures does James use to communicate the tongue's power to do both good and evil?

2. Why do you think James uses so many illustrations? Which word picture do you find most meaningful?

*3. James describes the untamed tongue as "a restless evil, full of deadly poison" (verse 8). Describe a time when you have seen the effects of that "deadly poison" in your life or in the life of someone you know.

4. In verse 2, James clearly states that we all stumble and fail to honor God in the things we say. He writes, *"If anyone is never at fault in what he says, he is a perfect man."* The Greek word for perfect is *teleos*, which means "mature" or "healthy." Who in your life demonstrates the greatest maturity with his or her tongue? Be specific about why you chose that person.

HOST TIP: ADDITIONAL QUESTIONS ARE PROVIDED AT THE END OF THIS LESSON FOR YOUR GROUP TO STUDY. DEPENDING ON THE SIZE OF YOUR GROUP, THE LENGTH OF TIME YOU'RE MEETING TOGETHER, AND/OR THE MEMBERS' LEVEL OF CHRISTIAN MATURITY, YOU MAY WANT TO USE THESE QUESTIONS AS SUGGESTED HOMEWORK EACH WEEK OR TURN THERE NOW FOR EXTENDED DISCUSSION.

Serve . . . . .15 minutes

*1. Describe a time when you were blessed by the words of someone who mattered to you. Contrast this with a time when you were hurt by another person's thoughtless words. What can you do to develop the habit of encouraging others with your words?

2. In what situations do you struggle most to control your own tongue? In conversations with your children? In hurtful moments with your parents? In disagreements with your spouse? Or some other place? What can the group do to help or support you?

Share . . . . .10 minutes

*1. Our speech can have a tremendous impact on the lives of unbelievers. 1 Peter 3:15b (NIV) says, *Always be prepared to give an answer to everyone who asks you to give the reason for the hope that you have. But do this with gentleness and respect*, . . . How do you respond to those who ask you about your faith? What have you learned about the importance of "gentleness and respect"?

2. Turn to the *Circles of Life* on page 74 in the *Small Group Resources* section. Use this tool to help you identify those around you who need to know Jesus. Make a plan to invite them to join you for your next meeting. As a group, pray this week for the people on your lists.

Worship . . . . .20 minutes

*1. We worship our heavenly Father not only with adoration and praise, but also with confession when we realize our sin. Have someone read aloud or sing together as a prayer the following praise chorus based on Psalm 51:10–12.

> *Create in me a clean heart, O God,*
> *And renew a right spirit within me.*
> *Create in me a clean heart, O God,*
> *And renew a right spirit within me.*
>
> *Cast me not away from Thy presence, O Lord,*
> *And take not Thy Holy Spirit from me.*
> *Restore unto me the joy of Thy salvation*
> *And renew a right spirit within me.*

Create in Me a Clean Heart, Author Unknown, Public Domain

2. Take time to pray for the requests of group members as well as for those people you want to invite to the next meeting. Record the needs and prayer requests of the group members on the *Small Group Prayer and Praise Report* (page 75 in the *Small Group Resources* section).

> HOST TIP: TO MAXIMIZE PRAYER TIME AND ALLOW GREATER OPPORTUNITY FOR PERSONAL SHARING, BREAK INTO SUBGROUPS OF THREE-TO-FOUR PEOPLE. THIS IS ESPECIALLY IMPORTANT IF YOUR GROUP IS MORE THAN EIGHT PEOPLE. WRITE PRAYER REQUESTS ON THE *SMALL GROUP PRAYER AND PRAISE REPORT*, PAGE 75.

Before You Leave

1. Take a few minutes to look at the *Small Group Calendar* (page 77 in the *Small Group Resources* section). Healthy groups share responsibilities and group ownership. Fill out the calendar together noting where you will meet each week, who will facilitate the discussion, and who will provide a meal or snack. Also note special events, socials, or days off. (Group Coordinator would be a great role for someone in your circle!)

2. Also, start collecting basic contact information like phone numbers and e-mail addresses. The group roster (called "My Small Group") on the inside front cover of this study guide is a good place to keep this information. Pass the study guides around the circle and have the members provide information about themselves.

Additional Study

1. According to Luke 6:45, what is the ultimate source of the things we say? What can we do to better control our tongues?

2. Read Titus 2:8. What does this verse say about the importance of speech in our witness to others? How would being in control of your tongue serve as an example of God's power in your life?

*3. In response to the question "What is the solution to controlling our tongue?" Pastor Rick shared three ideas. Which of these solutions—getting a new heart, asking God for help every day, and thinking before you speak—will you work on this week? Share both your answer and one practical step you hope to take this week with your group.

Preparation for Next Time

The Bible speaks frequently of wisdom. In the highly practical book of Proverbs, wisdom is exalted dozens of times. Therefore, it is imperative that Christians have a good understanding of this quality that God so highly prizes. In preparation for your next session, explore what the Bible teaches about wisdom.

1. During the week, read the *Daily Quiet Time Verses* listed in the inside back cover of this booklet. You might want to record your thoughts and note any direction you receive from the Lord in a journal.

2. Read James 3:13–18.

3. Read James 3:13 and Deuteronomy 4:6. According to these verses, what is clear evidence that a person possesses wisdom?

4. In Old Testament usage, the word *wise* described a person who had insight and skill for living. Such insight and skill grew out of the individual's relationship with God and his or her knowledge of God.

   • What definition of wisdom do you find in Job 28:28?

   • What does it mean to "fear the Lord"?

SESSION EIGHT:
HOW TO RELATE WISELY TO OTHERS
JAMES 3:13–18

HOST TIP: IF YOUR GROUP IS UNABLE TO WORK THROUGH ALL THE CURRICULUM, WE HAVE RECOMMENDED A QUESTION OR ACTIVITY WITH AN ASTERISK (*) IN EACH SECTION OF THE STUDY.

Connect . . . . .15 minutes

James begins the passage we are studying in this session by asking, *"Who is wise and understanding among you?"* (verse 13). *Wisdom* is one of those words that is difficult to define but fairly easy to recognize in someone's life. During this session we will examine the characteristics of a person who is wise in his or her relationships.

1. If anyone has joined your group this week, welcome each one and have everybody introduce themselves.

*2. Briefly describe someone you know who is wise in the way he or she relates to people. What specific incident revealed to you that person's wisdom?

Grow . . . . .45 minutes

Memory Verse
Who is wise and understanding among you? Let him show it by his good life,
by deeds done in the humility that comes from wisdom.
James 3:13 (NIV)

Watch the video now. Follow along in your Bibles and take notes on the provided outline.

¹³Who is wise and understanding among you? Let him show it by his good life, by deeds done in the humility that comes from wisdom. ¹⁴But if you harbor bitter envy and selfish ambition in your hearts, do not boast about it or deny the truth. ¹⁵Such "wisdom" does not come down from heaven but is earthly, unspiritual, of the devil. ¹⁶For where you have envy and selfish ambition, there you find disorder and every evil practice. ¹⁷But the wisdom that comes from heaven is first of all pure; then peace-loving, considerate, submissive, full of mercy and good fruit, impartial and sincere. ¹⁸Peacemakers who sow in peace raise a harvest of righteousness. (James 3:13–18 NIV)

- Wisdom is _____.

  Who is wise and understanding among you? Let him show it by his good life, . . . (James 3:13 NIV)

- A lack of wisdom causes _____.

1. If I'm wise, I won't compromise _____.

But the wisdom that comes from heaven is first of all pure; then peace-loving, considerate, submissive, full of mercy and good fruit, impartial and sincere. (James 3:17 NIV)

2. If I'm wise, I won't antagonize _____.

What causes arguments?

(1) _____

(2) _____

(3) _____

3. If I'm wise, I won't minimize _____ .

   Kind words bring life, but cruel words crush your spirit. (Proverbs 15:4 GN)

   Wisdom is _____ .

4. If I'm wise, I won't criticize _____ .

   But the wisdom that comes from heaven is . . . submissive, . . . (James 3:17 NIV)

   A fool thinks he needs no advice, but a wise man listens to others. (Proverbs 12:15 LB)

   Wisdom is _____ .

5. If I'm wise, I won't emphasize _____ .

   But the wisdom that comes from heaven is . . . full of mercy . . . (James 3:17 NIV)

   Love forgets mistakes; nagging about them parts the best of friends. (Proverbs 17:9 LB)

   Wisdom is _____ .

6. If I'm wise, I won't disguise _____ .

   But the wisdom that comes from heaven is . . . impartial and sincere. (James 3:17 NIV)

   You will never succeed in life if you try to hide your sins. (Proverbs 28:13a GN)

   Wisdom is _____ .

Discussion Questions

HOST TIP: IF YOUR GROUP HAS EIGHT OR MORE PEOPLE, GREATER PARTICIPATION AND DEEPER DISCUSSION MAY HAPPEN IF YOU BREAK INTO CIRCLES OF THREE OR FOUR PEOPLE. THEN COME BACK TOGETHER AT THE END OF THE DISCUSSION TIME AND HAVE SOMEONE FROM EACH CIRCLE REPORT THE HIGHLIGHTS OF THEIR DISCUSSION.

1. According to James 3:13, how do we know who is wise and understanding?

2. According to verse 14, what characteristics mark the person who is not led by godly wisdom?

3. James states that where there is *"envy and selfish ambition,"* you will find *"disorder and every evil practice"* (verse 16). What are some specific outward demonstrations of envy and selfish ambition?

*4. When James described wisdom that comes from God (verse 17), why do you think he listed purity first?

HOST TIP: ADDITIONAL QUESTIONS ARE PROVIDED AT THE END OF THIS LESSON FOR YOUR GROUP TO STUDY. DEPENDING ON THE SIZE OF YOUR GROUP, THE LENGTH OF TIME YOU'RE MEETING TOGETHER, AND/OR THE MEMBERS' LEVEL OF CHRISTIAN MATURITY, YOU MAY WANT TO USE THESE QUESTIONS AS SUGGESTED HOMEWORK EACH WEEK OR TURN THERE NOW FOR EXTENDED DISCUSSION.

Serve . . . . .10 minutes

Who doesn't want to live a life marked by godly wisdom! One of the most challenging areas in which to apply godly wisdom is in our relationships. But, as we read in James 1:5, if we lack wisdom, we *"should ask God, who gives generously."* Along with that call to prayer, James offers us some practical characteristics of wise living.

*1. The word *"submissive"* (verse 17) means "to be reasonable, willing to listen."
Read Proverbs 12:15 aloud. What positive steps can the group take to make sure every member feels listened to? (This practical advice works for relationships outside the group as well!)

*2. James 3:17 also states that the wisdom that comes from God is *"full of mercy."*
Read Proverbs 17:9 aloud. When someone in the group stumbles or struggles, what can other members do to show mercy?

Share . . . . .10 minutes

*1. Let's spend a few minutes evaluating ourselves against these six qualities of wise living. Fill out the following evaluation. Then name one quality in which you think you are doing well and one in which you need to grow.

Purity (honesty, integrity)	(Needs Work)	1	2	3	4	5	(Doing Well)
Peace-loving	(Needs Work)	1	2	3	4	5	(Doing Well)
Considerate (sensitive to others' feelings)	(Needs Work)	1	2	3	4	5	(Doing Well)
Submissive (open to reason)	(Needs Work)	1	2	3	4	5	(Doing Well)
Full of mercy and good fruit	(Needs Work)	1	2	3	4	5	(Doing Well)
Impartial and sincere	(Needs Work)	1	2	3	4	5	(Doing Well)

2. This week notice someone in your life who lives out the wisdom James describes. Encourage and affirm that person.

3. Prayerfully consider whether you need to talk with anyone to resolve a relational conflict. Ask the group to keep you accountable to resolving that conflict as soon as possible.

 Worship . . . .**15 minutes**

*1. As you close your meeting today, pray for the relationships among your group members. Also ask for prayer requests which group members may be struggling with concerning relationships outside the group.

2. Before you conclude, prayerfully commit yourselves to living out the six qualities of wisdom—pure, peace-loving, considerate, submissive, full of mercy and good fruit, impartial and sincere (verse 17).

*3. Close your time by praying for the needs of your group members. Record those prayer requests on the *Small Group Prayer and Praise Report* (page 75 in the *Small Group Resources* section).

Additional Study

*1. Proverbs 8:19 (NIV) says, *"My fruit is better than fine gold; what I yield surpasses choice silver."* Take a few moments to think about the "fruit" of wisdom. List fruit that comes out of a life of wisdom.

- Healthy relationships _____

- _____

- _____

- _____

2. The word *pure* means "uncorrupted" or "authentic." It is the quality of integrity. Proverbs 10:9a (NIV) states, *"The man of integrity walks securely, . . ."* Explain what this verse means.

3. In James 3:17, the words *impartial* and *sincere* come from two Greek words that sound very similar. Both are related to our word, *hypocrite*. In Greek theater, actors held masks in front of their faces to play different roles. The word that gave us *hypocrite* referred to these masks. Why do you think people wear "masks" to hide who they really are?

4. Read Proverbs 4:5–7 (NIV). Twice in these verses Solomon admonishes us to *"get wisdom."* What do these verses suggest about the importance of pursuing wisdom?

Preparation for Next Time

1. During the week, read the *Daily Quiet Time Verses* listed in the inside back cover of this booklet. You might want to record your thoughts and note any direction you receive from the Lord in a journal.

2. Read James 4:1–12.

3. According to Psalm 12:3, what are two things the Lord wants you to avoid? Which of these, if either, is especially difficult for you?

4. What is your reaction to Matthew 12:36?

9

SESSION NINE: HOW TO AVOID ARGUMENTS

JAMES 4:1–10

Connect . . . .**15 minutes**

*1. An accountability partner can help us stay on track with the Lord and provide an opportunity to grow spiritually. So take a moment to pair up with someone in your group to be spiritual partners for the remainder of this study. (We strongly recommend that men partner with men, women partner with women, or spouse with spouse.) Plan to check in with each other during the week by phone or e-mail, but take a minute now to talk about how wisely you related to others this past week. What opportunity did you have to put into practice something you learned from Session Eight?

2. Describe a situation from your teenage years when a parent or friend blew up initially but then worked with you to resolve the conflict.

 Grow . . . .**45 minutes**

Memory Verse
"God opposes the proud but gives grace to the humble."
James 4:6b (NIV)

Watch the video now. Follow along in your Bibles and take notes on the provided outline.

¹What causes fights and quarrels among you? Don't they come from your desires that battle within you? ²You want something but don't get it. You kill and covet, but you cannot have what you want. You quarrel and fight. You do not have, because you do not ask God. ³When you ask, you do not receive, because you ask with wrong motives, that you may spend what you get on your pleasures. ⁴You adulterous people, don't you know that friendship with the world is hatred toward God? Anyone who chooses to be a friend of the world becomes an enemy of God. ⁵Or do you think Scripture says without reason that the spirit he caused to live in us envies intensely? ⁶But he gives us more grace. That is why Scripture says: "God opposes the proud but gives grace to the humble." ⁷Submit yourselves, then, to God. Resist the devil, and he will flee from you. ⁸Come near to God and he will come near to you. Wash your hands, you sinners, and purify your hearts, you double-minded. ⁹Grieve, mourn and wail. Change your laughter to mourning and your joy to gloom. ¹⁰Humble yourselves before the Lord, and he will lift you up. (James 4:1–10 NIV)

1. The cause of all arguments is _____ .

What causes fights and quarrels among you? Don't they come from your desires that battle within you? (James 4:1 NIV)

Three basic desires cause arguments:

* The desire _____ (possessions)

  You want something but don't get it. You kill and covet, but you cannot have what you want . . . (James 4:2 NIV)

* The desire _____ (pleasure)

  When you ask, you do not receive, because you ask with wrong motives, that you may spend what you get on your pleasures. (James 4:3 NIV)

* The desire _____ (pride or power)

  Pride leads to arguments; be humble, take advice, and become wise. (Proverbs 13:10 LB)

  But he gives us more grace. That is why Scripture says: "God opposes the proud but gives grace to the humble." (James 4:6 NIV)

2. **The cure for arguments is** _____.

⁶But he gives us more grace. That is why Scripture says: "God opposes the proud but gives grace to the humble." ⁷Submit yourselves, then, to God. Resist the devil, and he will flee from you. ⁸Come near to God and he will come near to you. . . . ¹⁰Humble yourselves before the Lord, and he will lift you up. (James 4:6–8, 10 NIV)

Steps to defusing conflict

• _____.

Submit yourselves, then, to God. (James 4:7a NIV)

• _____.

Resist the devil, and he will flee from you. (James 4:7b NIV)

. . . in order that Satan might not outwit us. For we are not unaware of his schemes. (2 Corinthians 2:11 NIV)

• _____.

Come near to God and he will come near to you. (James 4:8a NIV)

He will keep in perfect peace all those who trust in him, whose thoughts turn often to the Lord! (Isaiah 26:3 LB)

• _____.

Wash your hands, you sinners, and purify your hearts, . . . (James 4:8b NIV)

Let there be tears for the wrong things you have done. (James 4:9a LB)

Discussion Questions

1. According to James 4:1, what is the root of our conflicts with others? When has an issue you've been battling in your heart spilled over into your actions or relationships?

2. Isaiah 26:3 says that God provides peace to all those who trust him. According to James 4:2–3, why do we find it difficult to trust God with areas of conflict?

*3. With which of the three desires that lead to conflict (possessions, pleasure, and pride) do you struggle the most? Why?

4. Each of the steps outlined for defusing conflict in our lives requires our willingness to humble ourselves before God. Briefly tell about a time when you humbled yourself and took a step toward resolving a conflict.

Serve . . . . 15 minutes

*1. Did anyone come to mind when Pastor Rick asked you to think of a person with whom you are in conflict right now? Without identifying the person, describe the situation. Which step—giving yourself to God, getting wise to Satan, growing closer to God, or asking forgiveness—do you need to take to resolve the situation? Are you willing to take that step? (You may want to pair up or gather in groups of three or four people for this discussion.)

Share . . . . 10 minutes

1. The way you handle conflict has a direct impact on your Christian testimony. Are you currently in a relational conflict with a non-Christian? How can you work to resolve that conflict in a way that will reflect the character of Christ? What will be your first step toward peace?

Worship . . . . 10 minutes

1. Take a few minutes to pray for those in your group who have described different relational conflicts in their lives. Pray that God will give them courage and wisdom as they work toward reconciliation and peace.

*2. Close your time by praying for the needs of your group members. Record those prayer requests on the *Small Group Prayer and Praise Report* (page 75 in the *Small Group Resources* section).

Additional Study

*1. Colossians 3:15a (NIV) says, *"Let the peace of Christ rule in your hearts . . ."* Are you letting Christ's peace rule in your heart? Are there any places in your heart where you have locked the door against the peace Christ wants to give?

2. Pastor Rick spoke of times when he and his wife Kay have experienced conflict and have done their best to resolve it. What conflict(s) have you needed to resolve in your own life? Give an example or two.

Preparation for Next Time

Americans spend billions of dollars trying to anticipate the future. Every night a significant portion of the newscast is dedicated to forecasting the weather. Expert stockbrokers and market analysts try to predict what will happen on Wall Street. And retailers spend millions trying to anticipate consumer buying trends. The reality is, none of us can know the future. In preparation for next week, see what God says about looking to the future.

1. During the week, read the *Daily Quiet Time Verses* listed in the inside back cover of this booklet. You might want to record your thoughts and note any direction you receive from the Lord in a journal.

2. Read James 4:13–17.

3. Read Matthew 6:25–34.

- We often fall into the trap of worrying about the future. But what do these verses promise the children of God?

- According to verse 30, what are we lacking when we worry about the future?

- According to verse 33, instead of being anxious about the future, in what should we invest our energy?

- In verse 34, Jesus seems to be saying that we should take care of today instead of worrying about tomorrow. In what ways would your life and attitude be different if you actually did live one day at a time?

4. Read Luke 12:16–21. What tragic mistakes did this man make?

10

SESSION TEN:
HOW TO FACE
YOUR FUTURE
JAMES 4:13–17

Connect . . . . .10 minutes

James now turns to a discussion of the future. How should Christians plan for the future? We have our Day-Timers®, our Palms® products, and our computer calendars, but is that kind of planning presumptuous? What does God have to say about how we make our plans? And how do our plans and God's plans for us fit together? These are fair questions, and in this session we will look to the Bible to help us answer them.

*1. Just as a regular medical checkup is a good way to measure physical health and spot potential problems, a spiritual checkup is vital to your spiritual well-being. The *Purpose Driven Health Assessment* (found on page 78 in the *Small Group Resources* section) was designed to give you a quick snapshot of your spiritual health. Take three or four minutes alone to answer the questions and tally your results. Then pair up with another person (preferably your spiritual partner) and briefly share a strength that you identified and an area where you would like to grow. Turn to the *Purpose Driven Health Plan* (page 80 in the *Small Group Resources* section) and, next to the purpose you want to work on, note a strategic step you could take.

2. Describe a time when God unexpectedly took your life in a different direction than you had planned.

Grow . . . . .45 minutes

Memory Verse
Anyone, then, who knows the good he ought to do and doesn't do it, sins.
James 4:17 (NIV)

Watch the video now. Follow along in your Bibles and take notes on the provided outline.

¹³Now listen, you who say, "Today or tomorrow we will go to this or that city, spend a year there, carry on business and make money." ¹⁴Why, you do not even know what will happen tomorrow. What is your life? You are a mist that appears for a little while and then vanishes. ¹⁵Instead, you ought to say, "If it is the Lord's will, we will live and do this or that." ¹⁶As it is, you boast and brag. All such boasting is evil. ¹⁷Anyone, then, who knows the good he ought to do and doesn't do it, sins. (James 4:13–17 NIV)

Three Common Mistakes to Avoid

Mistake #1: _____

Now listen, you who say, "Today or tomorrow we will go to this or that city, spend a year there, carry on business and make money." (James 4:13 NIV)

The Solution: _____.

Instead, you ought to say, "If it is the Lord's will, we will live and do this or that." (James 4:15 NIV)

Three Responses to God's Will:

- We can make a _____ to God's will.

- We can show _____ to God's will.

- We can show _____ for God's will.

  We should make plans—counting on God to direct us. (Proverbs 16:9 LB)

Mistake #2: _____

14 Why, you do not even know what will happen tomorrow. What is your life? You are a mist that appears for a little while and then vanishes. 15 Instead, you ought to say, "If it is the Lord's will, we will live and do this or that." (James 4:14–15 NIV)

Don't presume because . . .

• Life is _____ .

• Life is _____ .

> *"Come," each one cries, ". . . Let us drink our fill of beer! And tomorrow will be like today, or even far better." (Isaiah 56:12 NIV)*

> *Do not boast about tomorrow, for you do not know what a day may bring forth. (Proverbs 27:1 NIV)*

The Solution: _____ .

So don't be anxious about tomorrow. God will take care of your tomorrow too. Live one day at a time. (Matthew 6:34 LB)

Mistake #3: _____

Anyone, then, who knows the good he ought to do and doesn't do it, sins. (James 4:17 NIV)

Right now God is ready to welcome you. Today he is ready to save you. (2 Corinthians 6:2b LB)

27 Do not withhold good from those who deserve it, when it is in your power to act. 28 Do not say to your neighbor, "Come back later; I'll give it tomorrow"—when you now have it with you. (Proverbs 3:27–28 NIV)

The Solution: _____ .

Discussion Questions

1. We live in a culture that prizes efficient organization and carefully thought-out plans. We might commend the man mentioned in James 4:13, but James does not. What is missing from the plans mentioned in verse 13?

2. Read James 4:14 and Proverbs 27:1 aloud. According to these verses, why is it presumptuous to put too much confidence in our plans?

3. James states that life is uncertain and brief. Take turns reading the following verses and note other word pictures the Bible uses to talk about life.

Verse	Word Picture
Psalm 39:5	_____
Psalm 144:4	_____
Job 7:7, 9	_____
Psalm 103:15–16	_____

*4. James says that leaving God out of our plans is to arrogantly assume the future is totally in our control. What does James 4:16 say about this kind of boasting? Do you think most Christians regard leaving God out of their plans as "evil"? Why or why not?

Serve . . . . .10 minutes

All of us would like to know what lies ahead. It is natural and desirable to make plans for our future. James reminds us, though, that a Christian must put God front and center in his or her plans and always submit to God's control and sovereignty.

1. What are some practical steps—steps that reflect a dependence on and submission to God—that Christians can take when making plans for the future?

2. Why is it so important to say, *"If it is the Lord's will,"* as we make our plans?

*3. Pastor Rick stated that all of us are just one heartbeat away from eternity. If you lived your life in light of that reality, in what ways would your life be different this week? Have you been putting off doing something you know you should do? Share one example.

Share . . . . .15 minutes

*1. Proverbs 3:27–28 encourages us to help our neighbor today. Who in your neighborhood, school, community, small group, or church family has a practical need? What can you do to help meet that need? Be specific—and then act!

2. Within a short drive of most churches are men, women, and children who live in a world totally different from the one most of the churchgoers themselves live in. These people are hungry or homeless; they are poor and needy; they have been battered or abused. And you, as a group, have the opportunity to make not just a temporary difference, but an eternal difference in their lives. Discuss ways that you might like to get involved. Select a person to research the various outreach opportunities in your community that your group can do together. Then plan a day to reach out to the community around you.

Worship . . . . .10 minutes

As you wrap up your meeting, consider these ideas for your prayer time.

1. Spend time praying about the future of your group. What does God want your group to do next?

*2. Invite prayer requests from individuals who are concerned about their future. Consider praying for each person as he or she shares a specific request before moving on to the next person. Record those prayer requests on the *Small Group Prayer and Praise Report* (page 75 in the *Small Group Resources* section).

Additional Study

*1. Explain the relationship between James 4:17 and the four verses that precede it, verses 13–16. What is the "good" that the recipients of James' letter should have been doing?

2. Read Isaiah 40:21–26. What do these verses communicate about God's power and sovereignty over human affairs? When you think about your life and your future in light of these verses, how do you feel?

Preparation for Next Time

Americans are enamored with the lifestyles of the rich and famous, yet compared to the first century and to the rest of the world today, every person in your small group could be considered wealthy. While the Bible never condemns wealth or financial prosperity, it does warn against the potential dangers that come with wealth. In the passage we will study in our next session, James confronts some of the abuses of money that had crept into the church. We'll also look at what the Bible says about properly managing our financial resources.

1. During the week, read the *Daily Quiet Time Verses* listed in the inside back cover of this booklet. You might want to record your thoughts and note any direction you receive from the Lord in a journal.

2. Carefully read James 5:1–6. If James were speaking to your group in person, what tone of voice do you think he would use?

3. Read 1 Timothy 6:6–10.

   • Take a moment to honestly assess the level of your contentment. Read Ecclesiastes 5:10 and Matthew 6:19–21. In what ways does the attraction of materialism manifest itself in your life? Be specific.

   • Describe a few ways that the desire to get rich can be a trap leading to *"ruin and destruction"* (1 Timothy 6:9 NIV).

   • Why can money cause us to *"wander from the faith"* (1 Timothy 6:10 NIV)?

4. Read Matthew 19:16–26.

- In verse 21, Jesus is not saying that selling your possessions will get you into heaven. He is pointing out that this man's wealth had control of him and he was unwilling to love God more than his riches. Which of your riches, if any, interfere with your ability to love God with all your heart, soul, mind, and strength?

- In verse 23, Jesus states that it is hard for a rich man to enter the kingdom of heaven. Why is this so?

5. Read Proverbs 3:9–10. Write out what it would look like for you to *"honor the Lord with your wealth."* Then spend a few moments prayerfully and thankfully acknowledging God as the Owner of everything you have. Recognize that he has entrusted you to be a steward over his resources.

11

SESSION ELEVEN:
HOW TO BE WISE WITH
YOUR WEALTH

JAMES 5:1-6

Connect . . . . .15 minutes

Perhaps there is no more personal and sensitive topic than our money. In fact, it's tempting to avoid talking about this topic because it can make us all a little uncomfortable.

However, if we are to be fully devoted followers of Jesus, we must bring our personal finances under the scrutiny of Scripture. James involves us in a very straightforward discussion about how we use our money.

*1. Who handled the finances in your home when you were growing up? What attitudes toward money did you see in your parents?

Grow . . . . .45 minutes

Memory Verse
For where your treasure is, there your heart will be also.
Matthew 6:21 (NIV)

Watch the video now. Follow along in your Bibles and take notes on the provided outline.

¹Now listen, you rich people, weep and wail because of the misery that is coming upon you. ²Your wealth has rotted, and moths have eaten your clothes. ³Your gold and silver are corroded. Their corrosion will testify against you and eat your flesh like fire. You have hoarded wealth in the last days. ⁴Look! The wages you failed to pay the workmen who mowed your fields are crying out against you. The cries of the harvesters have reached the ears of the Lord Almighty. ⁵You have lived on earth in luxury and self-indulgence. You have fattened yourselves in the day of slaughter. ⁶You have condemned and murdered innocent men, who were not opposing you. (James 5:1–6 NIV)

Four Common Misuses of Wealth

1. Don't _____.

Your gold and silver are corroded. Their corrosion will testify against you and eat your flesh like fire. You have hoarded wealth in the last days. (James 5:3 NIV)

Your wealth has rotted, and moths have eaten your clothes. (James 5:2 NIV)

2. Don't _____.

The wages you have failed to pay the workmen who mowed your fields are crying out against you. (James 5:4a NIV)

3. Don't _____.

You have lived on earth in luxury and self-indulgence. (James 5:5a NIV)

4. Don't _____.

You have condemned and murdered innocent men who were not opposing you. (James 5:6 NIV)

The Right Uses of Wealth

1. _____ .

The wise man saves for the future, but the foolish man spends whatever he gets. (Proverbs 21:20 LB)

How to Save

• Learn to live on a _____

• Learn to be _____

Why Do Christians Save?

• Prevents us from _____

• Allows us to have _____

• Lets your money _____

2. _____ .

Wealth from gambling quickly disappears; wealth from hard work grows. (Proverbs 13:11 LB)

All hard work brings a profit, but mere talk leads only to poverty. (Proverbs 14:23 NIV)

Four Biblical Conditions for Earning Wealth

(1) Does not harm _____

> *Do not wear yourself out to get rich; have the wisdom to show restraint.*
> (Proverbs 23:4 NIV)

(2) Does not harm _____

(3) Does not harm _____

> *It is better to have a little, honestly earned, than to have a large income,*
> *dishonestly gained.* (Proverbs 16:8 GN)

(4) Does not harm _____

> *Beloved, I pray that in all respects you may prosper and be in good health,*
> *just as your soul prospers.* (3 John 2 NASB)

3. _____ .

The plans of the diligent lead to profit as surely as haste leads to poverty.
(Proverbs 21:5 NIV)

4. _____ .

It is possible to give away and become richer! It is also possible to hold on too tightly
and lose everything. Yes, the liberal man shall be rich! By watering others, he waters
himself. (Proverbs 11:24–25 LB)

On every Lord's Day each of you should put aside something from what you have
earned during the week, and use it for this offering. The amount depends on how
much the Lord has helped you earn . . . (1 Corinthians 16:2 LB)

Discussion Questions

1. What is the key point of James 5:2–3? Also, what is the difference between saving and hoarding (verse 3)?

2. Take turns reading the following verses aloud:

   Leviticus 19:13
   Deuteronomy 25:15–16
   Jeremiah 22:13
   Amos 8:4–7
   James 5:4

   What do these verses teach us about God's view of ethics in business? Do you feel pressure to participate in unethical business practices? If so, what do you do to stand strong against the pressure?

3. Why does James compare a luxurious and self-indulgent lifestyle to being *"fattened . . . in the day of slaughter"* (verse 5)?

*4. Read the following verses aloud. What does each say about the benefits of a strong work ethic?

Proverbs 12:27

Proverbs 14:23

Ephesians 6:5–8

1 Thessalonians 4:11–12

2 Thessalonians 3:10–12

5. When does a strong work ethic cross the line into "workaholism"?

Serve ....10 minutes

Jesus had a great deal to say about money and wealth. In his day as well as ours, his message about money was countercultural, yet his teaching offers the only way to true financial freedom.

1. As you think about your financial life, what is one area you feel good about? What is one area in which you need to grow?

*2. Pastor Rick identified four potential misuses of money:

 • An unhealthy accumulation of possessions
 • Cutting ethical corners in business practices
 • Careless spending
 • Using money to manipulate others

Have any of these been a struggle for you? How can your group members pray for you?

3. Sometime this week write out a prayer acknowledging God as Owner of all you possess. Also honestly examine to what degree you are controlled by a desire for more wealth and possessions. Ask God to give you contentment and to free you from bondage to material things.

Share . . . . .10 minutes

*1. Giving generously is one of the right uses of wealth—and compared to the rest of the world, each one of us is wealthy. So discuss as a group how giving to the church, to the poor and needy, to evangelism, and to world missions has blessed your life and turned your focus away from materialism. Plan to make a financial gift to help meet the needs in one of the categories just mentioned. Let your group or your spiritual partner know what step you plan to take.

2. Practice being generous this week. In faith, meet a need in someone else's life and do so anonymously. (Read Matthew 6:3–4 to discover what God promises when we do this!)

 Worship . . . . .15 minutes

As you close the meeting with prayer for your group, remember the importance of confidentiality. This session's topic is very personal, and people will share only if they feel the group is a safe place.

*1. Pray for group members struggling in the area of finances. (You might want to break the group into two or three smaller groups for your prayer time.)

*2. Close your time by praying for the needs of your group members. Record those prayer requests on the *Small Group Prayer and Praise Report* (page 75 in the *Small Group Resources* section).

Additional Study

*1. Read Proverbs 11:24–25; Luke 6:38; and Malachi 3:10. What does God promise those who give generously?

2. Read Proverbs 6:6–11. What commands for diligence and hard work do you find here?

Preparation for Next Time

1. During the week, read the *Daily Quiet Time Verses* listed in the inside back cover of this booklet. You might want to record your thoughts and note any direction you receive from the Lord in a journal.

2. Read James 5:7–20.

3. Read Hebrews 11 noting the number of times the phrase "by faith" appears. Which two or three examples of faith are most striking to you personally? Why?

4. Reread James 1:2–5. In light of developing patience through prayer, what does this passage teach you? What role do you think prayer plays in becoming more spiritually mature?

5. Confessing your sins and praying for one another offers the promise of healing. As Pastor Rick says, "Revealing your feelings is the beginning of healing."

   • What do you need to confess to God today?

   • What do you need to confess to someone else?

   • What, if anything, do you need to confess to your group?

12

SESSION TWELVE:
HOW TO DEVELOP PATIENCE THROUGH PRAYER
JAMES 5:7-20

Connect . . . . .15 minutes

*1. This is the last session in Volume Two of the study of James. We want to encourage you to review the *Purpose Driven Group Guidelines* (page 72). Discuss how the sessions have gone and any changes you would like to make. Talk about what you would like to study next, who will lead, and where you will meet. We invite you to visit our website at *www.purposedriven.com* to find more video-based small group studies. If you are planning to have an additional session for a social gathering, be sure everyone knows the details.

*2. Some people are able to be patient with any person, any problem, and any circumstance in their lives. Other people are quite the opposite. Rate your patience level on a scale of 1–10.

Personal Patience Scale

Everything happens too
slowly (low patience)   1 2 3 4 5 6 7 8 9 10   Easy come, easy go
(high patience)

Grow . . . . .45 minutes

Memory Verse
*Therefore confess your sins to each other and pray for
each other so that you may be healed.*
James 5:16a (NIV)

Watch the video now. Follow along in your Bibles and take notes on the provided outline.

⁷Be patient, then, brothers, until the Lord's coming. See how the farmer waits for the land to yield its valuable crop and how patient he is for the autumn and spring rains. ⁸You too, be patient and stand firm, because the Lord's coming is near. ⁹Don't grumble against each other, brothers, or you will be judged. The Judge is standing at the door! ¹⁰Brothers, as an example of patience in the face of suffering, take the prophets who spoke in the name of the Lord. ¹¹As you know, we consider blessed those who have persevered. You have heard of Job's perseverance and have seen what the Lord finally brought about. The Lord is full of compassion and mercy.
¹²Above all, my brothers, do not swear—not by heaven or by earth or by anything else. Let your "Yes" be yes, and your "No," no, or you will be condemned. ¹³Is any one of you in trouble? He should pray. Is anyone happy? Let him sing songs of praise. ¹⁴Is any one of you sick? He should call the elders of the church to pray over him and anoint him with oil in the name of the Lord. ¹⁵And the prayer offered in faith will make the sick person well; the Lord will raise him up. If he has sinned, he will be forgiven. ¹⁶Therefore confess your sins to each other and pray for each other so that you may be healed. The prayer of a righteous man is powerful and effective. ¹⁷Elijah was a man just like us. He prayed earnestly that it would not rain, and it did not rain on the land for three and a half years. ¹⁸Again he prayed, and the heavens gave rain, and the earth produced its crops. ¹⁹My brothers, if one of you should wander from the truth and someone should bring him back, ²⁰remember this: Whoever turns a sinner from the error of his way will save him from death and cover over a multitude of sins. (James 5:7–20 NIV)

When to Be Patient

- When circumstances are _____

  See how the farmer waits for the land to yield its valuable crop and how patient he is for the autumn and spring rains. (James 5:7b NIV)

- When people are _____

  Brothers, as an example of patience in the face of suffering, take the prophets who spoke in the name of the Lord. (James 5:10 NIV)

- When problems are _____

  As you know, we consider blessed those who have persevered. You have heard of Job's perseverance and have seen what the Lord finally brought about. (James 5:11 NIV)

Why Be Patient?

- Because _____

You too, be patient and stand firm, because the Lord's coming is near. (James 5:8 NIV)

- Because _____

As you know, we consider blessed those who have persevered. (James 5:11a NIV)

When Should I Pray?

- When I am _____

Is any one of you in trouble? He should pray. (James 5:13a NIV)

- When I am _____

[14]Is any one of you sick? He should call the elders of the church to pray over him and anoint him with oil in the name of the Lord. [15]And the prayer offered in faith will make the sick person well; the Lord will raise him up. If he has sinned, he will be forgiven. (James 5:14–15 NIV)

Three Kinds of Sickness

- Sickness unto _____
- Sickness unto _____
- Sickness unto _____

- When I am _____

Therefore confess your sins to each other and pray for each other so that you may be healed. The prayer of a righteous man is powerful and effective. (James 5:16 NIV)

How Do You Pray for Each Other?

- _____ .

- Have the _____ .

When you ask, you do not receive, because you ask with wrong motives, that you may spend what you get on your pleasures. (James 4:3 NIV)

- Have a _____ .

Therefore confess your sins to each other and pray for each other so that you may be healed. The prayer of a righteous man is powerful and effective. (James 5:16 NIV)

- _____ .

But when he asks, he must believe and not doubt, . . . (James 1:6 NIV)

Discussion Questions

1. What does the illustration of the farmer in James 5:7 say about patience?

2. The prophets of the Bible were patient with people who were unwilling or even uninterested in changing. Tell of someone in your past (a parent, spouse, friend, etc.) who offered you that same kind of patience.

*3. The story of Job has been called the "Super Bowl of Suffering." This faithful man of God lost his family, friends, and finances suddenly and unexpectedly. Few of us will ever come close to experiencing such loss. Yet Job never challenged or cursed God, even though he was thoroughly confused about what God was doing in his life. According to James 5:11, what did Job believe about God that enabled him to persevere without cursing God?

4. In James 5:13–20, we who are God's people are encouraged to pray when we are in trouble and to confess our sins to one another. What benefits do we receive when we do this?

 Serve . . . .**15 minutes**

1. In what ways has your group shown you love, patience, or been persistent in praying for you? Take a few minutes to thank the group—and thank God for the group—now.

*2. When do you struggle most to be patient with God? With whom in your life do you struggle most to be patient? Have someone pray about the situation or relationship you just identified.

3. James 5:16 is a clear statement of our responsibility and personal need to confess our sins to one another. Do you need to be vulnerable and confess something that is disappointing to God? Or do you need to check in with a group member with whom you experience tension? The passage says that, as a result of confession, you (and your group) will be healed.

Share ....10 minutes

The prayer of a righteous man is powerful and effective. (James 5:16b NIV)

*1. Are you praying regularly for those you know who do not have a personal relationship with Jesus Christ? Take a moment and write down the names of three people you know who do not know Christ. They could be family members, friends, neighbors, or associates at work.

Names: _____ _____ _____

2. Make the commitment to pray for these people on a weekly basis. Set aside part of your prayer time to pray that God would open their hearts to him; that he would give you or other believers opportunities to talk with them about Jesus; and that they might come to know Christ personally as their Savior and Lord. Pray together for several of the people on your group members' lists.

Worship ....15 minutes

*1. When we read the Bible, we can all too easily keep on reading rather than stop to do what it says. We come to one such place in James 5:13b (NIV): *Is anyone happy? Let him sing songs of praise.* Many of us may read these words and continue to the next verse without a pause. Your group may be missing one of God's greatest blessings by not taking the time to celebrate his presence together. Why not close your meeting with a simple worship song that members of your group know well?

63

2. James teaches that the prayer of a righteous person is powerful and effective (5:16b). So select someone in your group who has a specific physical, emotional, or spiritual need and have the group lay hands on that person and pray. This could be one of the most significant times your group shares. May God use this time to teach you to, *"Rejoice with those who rejoice; mourn with those who mourn"* (Romans 12:15 NIV).

Additional Study

1. James 5:8 (NIV) says, *"be patient and stand firm, because the Lord's coming is near."* Why is this truth an encouragement to be more patient whatever the circumstances of your life? When has this particular verse encouraged you?

2. In James 5:16b (NIV), we read that the *"prayer of a righteous man is powerful and effective."* Where in the Bible do you see a believer's prayer being "powerful and effective"? Give a favorite example or two. When have believers' prayers been "powerful and effective" in your own life? Be specific. And when have the prayers of your small group been "powerful and effective"? Again, be specific.

GROUP DEVELOPMENT: SMALL GROUP RESOURCES

Helps for Hosts

Top Ten Ideas for New Hosts

Congratulations! As the Host of your small group, you have responded to the call to help shepherd Jesus' flock. Few other tasks in the family of God surpass the contribution you will be making.

As you prepare to facilitate your group, whether it is one session or the entire series, here are a few thoughts to keep in mind. We encourage you to read and review these tips with each new discussion host before he or she leads.

Remember you are not alone. God knows everything about you, and he knew you would be asked to facilitate your group. Even though you may not feel ready, this is common for all good hosts. God promises, *"I will never leave you; I will never abandon you"* (Hebrews 13:5 TEV). Whether you are facilitating for one evening, several weeks, or a lifetime, you will be blessed as you serve.

1. **Don't try to do it alone.** Pray right now for God to help you build a healthy team. If you can enlist a co-host to help you shepherd the group, you will find your experience much richer. This is your chance to involve as many people as you can in building a healthy group. All you have to do is ask people to help. You'll be surprised at the response.

2. **Be friendly and be yourself.** God wants to use your unique gifts and temperament. Be sure to greet people at the door with a big smile . . . this can set the mood for the whole gathering. Remember, they are taking as big a step as you are to show up at your house! Don't try to do things exactly like another host; do them in a way that fits you. Admit when you don't have an answer and apologize when you make a mistake. Your group will love you for it and you'll sleep better at night.

3. **Prepare for your meeting ahead of time.** Watch the video session before your group arrives. Write down your responses to each question. Pay special attention to exercises that ask group members to do something other than engage in discussion. These exercises will help your group live what the Bible teaches, not just talk about it. Be sure you understand how an exercise works. If the exercise employs one of the items in the *Small Group Resource* section (such as the *Group Guidelines*), be sure to look over that item so you'll know how it works.

4. **Pray for your group members by name.** Before you begin your session, take a few moments and pray for each member by name. You may want to review the prayer list at least once a week. Ask God to use your time together to touch the heart of every person in your group. Expect God to lead you to whomever he wants you to encourage or challenge in a special way. If you listen, God will surely lead.

5. **When you ask a question, be patient.** Someone will eventually respond. Sometimes people need a moment or two of silence to think about the question. If silence doesn't bother you, it won't bother anyone else. After someone responds, affirm the response with a simple "thanks" or "great answer." Then ask, "How about somebody else?" or "Would someone who hasn't shared like to add anything?" Be sensitive to new people or reluctant members who aren't ready to say, pray, or do anything. If you give them a safe setting, they will blossom over time. If someone in your group is a "wall flower" who sits silently through every session, consider talking to them privately and encouraging them to participate. Let them know how important they are to you—that they are loved and appreciated, and that the group would value their input. Remember, still water often runs deep.

6. **Provide transitions between questions.** Ask if anyone would like to read the paragraph or Bible passage. Don't call on anyone, but ask for a volunteer, and then be patient until someone begins. Be sure to thank the person who reads aloud.

7. **Break into smaller groups occasionally.** The Grow and Worship sections provide good opportunities to break into smaller circles of three to five people. With a greater opportunity to talk in a small circle, people will connect more with the study, apply more quickly what they're learning, and ultimately get more out of their small group experience. A small circle also encourages a quiet person to participate and tends to minimize the effects of a more vocal or dominant member.

8. **Small circles are also helpful during prayer time.** People who are unaccustomed to praying aloud will feel more comfortable trying it with just two or three others. Also, prayer requests won't take as much time, so circles will have more time to actually pray. When you gather back with the whole group, you can have one person from each circle briefly update everyone on the prayer requests from their subgroups. The other great aspect of subgrouping is that it fosters leadership development. As you ask people in the group to facilitate discussion or to lead a prayer circle, it gives them a small leadership step that can build their confidence.

9. **Rotate facilitators occasionally.** You may be perfectly capable of hosting each time, but you will help others grow in their faith and gifts if you give them opportunities to host the group.

10. **One final challenge (for new or first-time hosts).** Before your first opportunity to lead, look up each of the six passages listed below. Read each one as a devotional exercise to help prepare you with a shepherd's heart. Trust us on this one. If you do this, you will be more than ready for your first meeting.

Matthew 9:36–38

[36] When Jesus saw the crowds, he had compassion on them, because they were harassed and helpless, like sheep without a shepherd. [37] Then he said to his disciples, "The harvest is plentiful but the workers are few. [38] Ask the Lord of the harvest, therefore, to send out workers into his harvest field."

John 10:14–15

[14] I am the good shepherd; I know my sheep and my sheep know me—[15] just as the Father knows me and I know the Father—and I lay down my life for the sheep.

1 Peter 5:2–4

[2] Be shepherds of God's flock that is under your care, serving as overseers—not because you must, but because you are willing, as God wants you to be; [3] not greedy for money, but eager to serve; not lording it over those entrusted to you, but being examples to the flock. [4] And when the Chief Shepherd appears, you will receive the crown of glory that will never fade away.

Philippians 2:1–5

[1] If you have any encouragement from being united with Christ, if any comfort from his love, if any fellowship with the Spirit, if any tenderness and compassion, [2] then make my joy complete by being like-minded, having the same love, being one in spirit and purpose. [3] Do nothing out of selfish ambition or vain conceit, but in humility consider others better than yourselves. [4] Each of you should look not only to your own interests, but also to the interests of others. [5] Your attitude should be the same as that of Jesus Christ.

Hebrews 10:23–25

[23] Let us hold unswervingly to the hope we profess, for he who promised is faithful. [24] And let us consider how we may spur one another on toward love and good deeds. [25] Let us not give up meeting together, as some are in the habit of doing, but let us encourage one another—and all the more as you see the Day approaching.

1 Thessalonians 2:7–8, 11–12

[7] But we were gentle among you, like a mother caring for her little children. [8] We loved you so much that we were delighted to share with you not only the Gospel of God but our lives as well, because you had become so dear to us. . . . [11] For you know that we dealt with each of you as a father deals with his own children, [12] encouraging, comforting and urging you to live lives worthy of God, who calls you into his kingdom and glory.

Frequently Asked Questions

Who may attend group?

Anybody you feel would benefit. As you begin, we encourage each attendee to invite at least one other friend to join. The best time to have people join the group is in the first or second week of a new study. Take some time at your first meeting to share names of friends with group members so that as a group you can pray that they might be open to attend.

How long will this group meet?

This series is six weeks long, and we encourage groups to add one additional week for a celebration. At the end of this study, each group member may decide if he or she desires to continue on for another six-week study. In your final session take time to review your Group Agreement, and discuss what study you might do next. We recommend you visit our website at *www.purposedriven.com* for more video-based small group studies.

Who is the host?

The host is the person who coordinates and facilitates your group meetings. In addition to a host, we encourage you to select one or more group members to lead your group discussions. Several other responsibilities can be rotated, including refreshments, prayer requests, worship, or keeping up with those who miss a meeting. Shared ownership in the group helps everybody grow.

Where do we find new group members for our group?

This can be an issue for groups, especially new groups starting with just a few people or existing groups that lose a few people along the way. We encourage you to brainstorm a list of people from your work, church, neighborhood, children's school, family, the gym, and so on. Then pray for the people on each member's list. Have each group member invite several people on their list. No matter how you find members, it is important to continue actively looking for new people to join your group. All groups go through some healthy attrition as a result of moves, releasing new leaders, ministry opportunities, and so forth. If the group gets too small, it runs the risk of shutting down. Remember, the next person you add just might become a friend for eternity. You never know.

How do we handle the childcare needs in our group?

Childcare needs must be handled very carefully. This is a sensitive issue. We suggest you seek creative solutions as a group. One common solution is to have the adults meet in the living room and share the cost of a baby sitter (or two) who can be with the kids in another part of the house. Another popular option is to have one home for the kids and a second home (close by) for the adults. If desired, the adults could rotate the responsibility of providing a lesson for the kids. This last option is great with school age kids and can be a huge blessing to families.

What if we cannot get through all the content each week?

The curriculum is provided to serve you as a group and as a host. Do not feel obligated to get through all the content in this study guide. Be sensitive to the leading of the Holy Spirit during your group meeting. Some items will be more applicable for your group than others. Choose those items that best fit your group life. However, if an item stretches you as a group, do not ignore it. New experiences will breathe new growth and community into your small group.

Many groups are able to complete these study guides in the suggested six weeks, while others take several extra weeks. Please feel free to adjust your pace according to the needs of your group. If the need arises to take a week and give attention to needs in your group, do so. Then come back to the study guide the next week. We encourage you to periodically meet together specifically for the purpose of building relationships within your group.

Purpose Driven Group Guidelines

It's a good idea for every group to put words to their shared values, expectations, and commitments. Such guidelines will help you avoid unspoken agendas and unmet expectations. We recommend you discuss your guidelines during Session One in order to lay the foundation for a healthy group experience. Feel free to modify anything that does not work for your group.

If the idea of a written agreement is unfamiliar to your group, we encourage you to give it a try.

We agree to the following values:

Clear Purpose	To grow healthy spiritual lives by building a healthy small group community
Group Attendance	To give priority to the group meeting (call if I am absent or late)
Safe Environment	To create a safe place where people can be heard and feel loved (no quick answers, snap judgments, or simple fixes)
Be Confidential	To keep anything that is shared strictly confidential and within the group
Conflict Resolution	To avoid gossip and to immediately resolve any concerns by following the principles of Matthew 18:15–17
Spiritual Health	To give group members permission to speak into my life and help me live a healthy, balanced spiritual life that is pleasing to God
Limit Our Freedom	To limit our freedom by not serving or consuming alcohol during small group meetings or events so as to avoid causing a weaker brother or sister to stumble (1 Corinthians 8:1–13; Romans 14:19–21)
Welcome Newcomers	To invite friends who might benefit from this study and warmly welcome newcomers
Building Relationships	To get to know the other members of the group and pray for them regularly
Other	_____
	_____
	_____

Purpose Driven Group Agreement

We have also discussed and agree on the following items:

Child Care

_____

_____

Starting Time

_____

Ending Time

_____

If you haven't already done so, take a few minutes to fill out the *Small Group Calendar* on page 77.

Circles of Life—Small Group Connections

Discover who you can connect in community

Use this chart to help carry out one of the values in the *Purpose Driven Group Guidelines* and *Purpose Driven Group Agreement,* to "Welcome Newcomers."

"Come follow me . . . and I will make you fishers of men."
Matthew 4:19 (NIV)

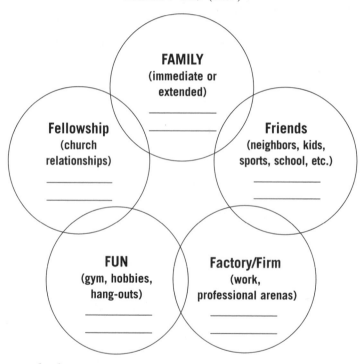

Follow this simple three-step process:

1. List one to two people in each circle.

2. Prayerfully select one person or couple from your list and tell your group about them.

3. Give them a call and invite them to your next meeting. Over fifty percent of those invited to a small group say, "Yes!"

Small Group Prayer and Praise Report

This is a place where you can write each other's requests for prayer. You can also make a note when God answers a prayer. Pray for each other's requests. If you're new to group prayer, it's okay to pray silently or to pray by using just one sentence: "God, please help

_____ to _____ ."

DATE	PERSON	PRAYER REQUEST	PRAISE REPORT

Small Group Prayer and Praise Report

DATE	PERSON	PRAYER REQUEST	PRAISE REPORT

Small Group Calendar

Healthy groups share responsibilities and group ownership. It might take some time for this to develop. Shared ownership ensures that responsibility for the group doesn't fall to one person. Use the calendar to keep track of social events, mission projects, birthdays, or days off. Complete this calendar at your first or second meeting. Planning ahead will increase attendance and shared ownership.

DATE	LESSON	LOCATION	FACILITATOR	SNACK OR MEAL
10/22	Session 2	Steve & Laura	Bill Jones	John & Alice

How the Assessment Works

The *Purpose Driven Health Assessment* is designed to help you evaluate how well you are balancing the five purposes in your life, and to identify your areas of strength and weakness. The Assessment consists of thirty-five statements that are linked to the five purposes.

Instructions

1. Rate yourself on each of the statements using a scale from 0 to 5, with zero meaning the statement does not match you and five meaning it is a very strong match for you.

2. After you have rated each statement, tally the results by transferring your ratings for each of the statements to the scoring table on this page. Then add up the numbers in each column to find your score for each purpose.

3. Turn to the *Purpose Driven Health Plan* on page 80 for further instructions.

My Spiritual Health Assessment

WORSHIP	FELLOWSHIP	DISCIPLESHIP	MINISTRY	EVANGELISM
1. _____	2. _____	3. _____	4. _____	5. _____
6. _____	7. _____	8. _____	9. _____	10. _____
11. _____	12. _____	13. _____	14. _____	15. _____
16. _____	17. _____	18. _____	19. _____	20. _____
21. _____	22. _____	23. _____	24. _____	25. _____
26. _____	27. _____	28. _____	29. _____	30. _____
31. _____	32. _____	33. _____	34. _____	35. _____
[ ]	[ ]	[ ]	[ ]	[ ]

Spiritual Health Assessment

		Doesn't Match	Partial Match	Strong Match

1. Pleasing God with my life is my highest priority. 0   1   2   3   4   5 .
2. I am genuinely open and honest about who I am with others. 0   1   2   3   4   5
3. I quickly confess anything in my character that does not look like Christ. 0   1   2   3   4   5
4. I often think about how to use my time more wisely to serve God. 0   1   2   3   4   5
5. I feel personal responsibility to share my faith with those who don't know Jesus. 0   1   2   3   4   5
6. I am dependent on God for every aspect of my life. 0   1   2   3   4   5
7. I regularly use my time and resources to care for the needs of others. 0   1   2   3   4   5
8. How I spend my time and money shows that I think more about God and others than I do about myself. . . 0   1   2   3   4   5
9. I am currently serving God with the gifts and passions he has given me. 0   1   2   3   4   5
10. I look for opportunities to build relationships with those who don't know Jesus. 0   1   2   3   4   5
11. There is nothing in my life that I have not surrendered to (kept back from) God. 0   1   2   3   4   5
12. I have a deep and meaningful connection with others in the church. 0   1   2   3   4   5
13. I allow God's Word to guide my thoughts and change my actions. 0   1   2   3   4   5
14. I regularly reflect on how my life can have an impact for the Kingdom of God. 0   1   2   3   4   5
15. I regularly pray for those who don't know Christ. 0   1   2   3   4   5 .
16. I regularly meditate on God's Word and invite him into my everyday activities. 0   1   2   3   4   5
17. I have an easy time allowing someone who knows me to speak truth to me. 0   1   2   3   4   5
18. I am able to praise God during difficult times and see them as opportunities to grow. 0   1   2   3   4   5
19. I often think about ways to use my God-given SHAPE to please God. 0   1   2   3   4   5
20. I am confident in my ability to share my faith. 0   1   2   3   4   5
21. I have a deep desire to be in God's presence and spend time with him. 0   1   2   3   4   5
22. I gather regularly with a group of Christians for fellowship and accountability. 0   1   2   3   4   5
23. I find I am making more choices that cause me to grow when I am tempted to do wrong. 0   1   2   3   4   5
24. I enjoy meeting the needs of others without expecting anything in return. 0   1   2   3   4   5
25. My heart is full of passion to share the good news of the gospel with those who have never heard it. 0   1   2   3   4   5
26. I am the same person at church that I am in private. 0   1   2   3   4   5
27. There is nothing in my relationships that is currently unresolved. 0   1   2   3   4   5
28. I have found that prayer has changed how I view and interact with the world. 0   1   2   3   4   5
29. Those closest to me would say my life is a reflection of giving more than receiving. 0   1   2   3   4   5
30. I find that my relationship with Jesus comes up frequently in my conversations with those who 0   1   2   3   4   5
don't know him.
31. I have an overwhelming sense of God's awesomeness even when I do not feel his presence. 0   1   2   3   4   5
32. There is nothing in the way I talk or act concerning others that I would not be willing to share with 0   1   2   3   4   5
them in person.
33. I am consistent in pursuing habits that are helping me model my life after Jesus. 0   1   2   3   4   5
34. I am open about my weaknesses and see them as opportunities to minister to others. 0   1   2   3   4   5
35. I am open to going anywhere God calls me in whatever capacity to share my faith. 0   1   2   3   4   5

Purpose Driven Health Plan

After completing the *Purpose Driven Health Assessment*, focus on the areas with lower scores or where you feel you need to plan for growth, and complete this *Purpose Driven Health Plan*. Fill in the possible ideas for developing your spiritual life in each area, then translate those possibilities into actual steps you plan to take to grow or develop in each purpose.

Purposes	Possibilities	Plans (Strategic Steps)
CONNECT (Fellowship) How can I deepen my relationships with others? • Family/friends • Relational/emotional development • Small group community		
GROW (Discipleship) How can I grow to be like Christ? • Spiritual disciplines • Financial stewardship • Character development		
SERVE (Ministry) How can I serve God and others? • Ministry to the Body • Leadership training • Continuing training		
SHARE (Evangelism) How can I share my faith regularly? • Mission to the world • Seeker friends/family, work, neighborhood involvement		
WORSHIP How can I live for God's pleasure? • Regular church attendance • Worship tapes and devotionals • Personal health and balance		

Answer Key

Session Seven—How to Manage Your Mouth

My tongue directs <u>where I go</u>.
My tongue can destroy <u>what I have</u>.
My tongue displays <u>who I am</u>.
The problem is with <u>your heart</u>.
<u>Get a new heart</u>.
<u>Ask God for help every day</u>.
<u>Think before you speak</u>.

Session Eight—How to Relate Wisely to Others

Wisdom is <u>a lifestyle</u>.
A lack of wisdom causes <u>problems</u>.
If I'm wise, I won't compromise <u>my integrity</u>.
If I'm wise, I won't antagonize <u>your anger</u>.
<u>Comparing</u>
<u>Condemning</u>
<u>Contradicting</u>
If I'm wise, I won't minimize <u>your feelings</u>.
Wisdom is <u>considerate</u>.
If I'm wise, I won't criticize <u>your suggestions</u>.
Wisdom is <u>submissive</u>.
If I'm wise, I won't emphasize <u>your mistakes</u>.
Wisdom is <u>full of mercy</u>.
If I'm wise, I won't disguise <u>my feelings</u>.
Wisdom is <u>impartial and sincere</u>.

Session Nine—How to Avoid Arguments

The cause of all arguments is <u>conflict and desires</u>.
The desire <u>to have</u> (possessions)
The desire <u>to feel</u> (pleasure)
The desire <u>to be</u> (pride or power)
The cure for arguments is <u>humility</u>.
<u>Give yourself to God</u>.
<u>Get wise to Satan</u>.
<u>Grow closer to God</u>.
<u>Ask forgiveness</u>.

Session Ten—How to Face Your Future

Mistake #1: <u>Planning without God</u>
The Solution: <u>Include God in goal-setting</u>.
We can make a <u>reference</u> to God's will.
We can show <u>deference</u> to God's will.
We can show <u>preference</u> for God's will.
Mistake #2: <u>Presuming about tomorrow</u>

Life is <u>unpredictable</u>.
Life is <u>brief</u>.
The Solution: <u>Live one day at a time</u>.
Mistake #3: <u>Putting off doing good</u>
The Solution: <u>Do it now</u>.

Session Eleven—How to Be Wise with Your Wealth

Don't <u>hoard it</u>.
Don't <u>steal it</u>.
Don't <u>waste it</u>.
Don't <u>abuse it</u>.
<u>Save it faithfully</u>.
Learn to live on a <u>margin</u>.
Learn to be <u>content</u>.
Prevents us from <u>wasting money</u>
Allows us to have <u>money in reserve</u>
Lets your money <u>work for you</u>
<u>Make it honestly</u>.
<u>Your health</u>
<u>Your family</u>
<u>Other people</u>
<u>Spiritual life</u>
<u>Spend it wisely</u>.
<u>Give it generously</u>.

Session Twelve—How to Develop Patience through Prayer

When circumstances are <u>uncontrollable</u>
When people are <u>unchangeable</u>
When problems are <u>unexplainable</u>
Because <u>God is in control</u>
Because <u>God rewards patience</u>
When I am <u>hurting emotionally</u>
When I am <u>hurting physically</u>
Sickness unto <u>death</u>
Sickness unto <u>discipline</u>
Sickness unto <u>the glory of God</u>
When I am <u>hurting spiritually</u>
<u>Be specific</u>.
Have the <u>right motives</u>.
Have a <u>clean life</u>.
<u>Ask in faith</u>.

Memory Verses — One of the most effective ways to deepen our understanding of the principles we are learning in this series is to memorize key Scripture verses. For many, Bible memorization is a new concept or one that has been difficult in the past. But we encourage you to stretch yourself and try to memorize these six *Memory Verses*. If possible, memorize them as a group and make them part of your group time.

I have hidden your word in my heart that I might not sin against you.
Psalm 119:11 (NIV)

Session Seven

Let the peace of Christ rule in your hearts . . .

Colossians 3:15a (NIV)

Session Eight

Who is wise and understanding among you? Let him show it by his good life, by deeds done in the humility that comes from wisdom.

James 3:13 (NIV)

Session Nine

"God opposes the proud but gives grace to the humble."

James 4:6b (NIV)

Session Ten

Anyone, then, who knows the good he ought to do and doesn't do it, sins.

James 4:17 (NIV)

Session Eleven

For where your treasure is, there your heart will be also.

Matthew 6:21 (NIV)

Session Twelve

Therefore confess your sins to each other and pray for each other so that you may be healed.

James 5:16a (NIV)
